The Amazing Book of SCIENCE

ARCTURUS

Picture Credits:

Every attempt has been made to clear copyright. Should there be any inadvertent omission, please apply to the publisher for rectification.

Key: b–bottom, t–top, c–centre, l–left, r–right

Alamy: 26–27 (David Fleetham), 114–115 (Greg Vaughn), 115cr (Xinhua); **Science Photo Library:** 1 (Jellyfish Pictures), 4–5 (Photo Insolite Realite), 9cl (Tony McConnell), 10cl (Dr Gary Settles), 38–39 (Samuel Ashfield), 38cl (US Army), 40–41 (Nicolle R Fuller), 40cr (Philippe Plailly), 44cr (Planetary Visions Ltd), 45br (Spencer Sutton), 46cr (Henning Dalhoff); **Shutterstock:** cover main (Sebastian Kaulitzki), cover (top row, various), 4tr (adriaticfoto), 4c (Neal Pritchard Media), 4br (YC_Chee), 5tr (adike), 5br (NASA Images), 6–7 (ZinaidaSopina), 6tr (MicroOne), 6bl (sandatlas.org), 7bl (kaer_stock), 8–9 (Sebastian Janicki), 8cl (grafvision), 9bl (Macrovector), 10–11 (Digital Storm), 10bl (MilanMarkovic78), 11tl (Evgeniya Chertova), 12cr (Lightspring), 12bc (Susan Schmitz), 14–15 (hamdee), 14l (Calmara), 15cr (koya979), 16–17 (Brannon_Naito), 16cr (Sakura), 16br (Molly NZ), 17bl (BlueRingMedia), 18tr (tcareob72), 18trbl (hillmanchaiyaphum), 18trbr (Popova Tetiana), 18ct, 18ctr (schankz), 18c (Andrey Armyagov), 18cbr (F Neidl), 18cb (Gerald Robert Fischer), 18bl (dangdumrong), 18br (Jolanta Wojcicka), 19tlb (Romeo Andrei Cana), 19tc (Victor Tyakht), 19tr (Zety Akhzar), 19ct (Rich Carey), 19ctr (Salparadis), 19cb (scubaluna), 19bc (Rich Carey), 19br (Laura Dinraths), 20–21(Sirisak_baokaew), 20cr (Sebastian Kaulitzi), 20bl (eenoki), 20–21 (Life science), 22cl (Christos Georghiou), 22bl (NotionPic), 23br (VILevi), 24–25 (Biomedical), 24tr (NoPainNoGain), 24bl (stihii), 25bl (LynxVector), 26–27 (adike), 26tr (yodiyim), 26c (wavebreakmedia), 27bl (Tefi), 28–29 (Michal Knitl), 28cl (Tefi), 29cr (Robert J Gatto), 29bl (Everett Historical), 30–31 (Sebastian Kaulitzki), 30cl (deepadesigns), 30cr (Designua), 31cr (Sebastian Kaulitzki), 31bl (Panda Vector), 32–33 (Cassiohabib), 32cr (Roberto Cerruti), 32c (JonathanC Photography), 32bl (StockSmartStart), 33cr (Aspen Photo), 34–35(Gabor Kenyeres), 34tr (Littlekidmoment), 34c (SkyPics Studio), 34bl (Fouad A Saad), 36–37 (Kobby Dagan), 36cl (kasezo), 36bl (MatiasDelCarmine), 39tr (Volodymyr Krasyuk), 40tr (Forance), 40bl (Shmitt Maria), 42–43 (Vadim Sadovski/NASA), 42tr (Diego Barucco), 42cr (Marc Ward/NASA), 44–45 (Therato), 44bl (Palau), 46bl (robin2); **thehistoryblog.com:** 15bl; **Wellcome Images:** 21tl; **Wikimedia Commons:** 13tl (Alexander Roslin, Nationalmuseum, Stockholm, Sweden), 19tl (Maija Karala), 37tr (Niabot), 38bl (Science Museum, London/Mrjohncummings), 42bl (Davorka Herak and Marijan Herak).

In this book, one billion means one thousand million (1,000,000,000) and one trillion means one million million (1,000,000,000,000).

ARCTURUS

This edition published in 2019 by Arcturus Publishing Limited
26/27 Bickels Yard, 151–153 Bermondsey Street,
London SE1 3HA

Consultant: Dr. Mandy Hartley
Author: Giles Sparrow
Editors: Clare Hibbert and Samantha Hilton
Designers: Amy McSimpson and Trudi Webb

ISBN: 978-1-78950-837-6
CH007558UK
Supplier 29, Date 0719, Print run 9204

Printed in China

The Amazing Book of
SCIENCE

CONTENTS

Introduction

Science is amazing! It shapes our understanding of the Universe and has transformed our everyday lives. At its heart, science is a way of collecting facts, developing ideas to explain those facts, and making predictions we can test.

Laboratory Learning

Chemistry investigates materials, from solids, liquids, and gases to the tiny atoms that make up everything. By understanding the rules behind how different kinds of matter behave, we can create new chemicals and materials with amazing properties.

Observing a chemical reaction under a microscope

Secrets of the Universe

Physics is the scientific study of energy, forces, mechanics, and waves. Energy includes heat, light, and electricity. Physics also looks at the structure of atoms and the workings of the Universe. Even the galaxies obey the laws of physics!

Chimpanzees, one of around 7.8 million species of living animals

Many forms of energy are involved in a storm.

Life on Earth

Natural history is the study of living things—the countless plants, animals, and other creatures that inhabit Earth now or which existed in the past. It studies how these organisms are influenced by each other and their environment. It also looks at the complex process of evolution—gradual change from one generation to the next.

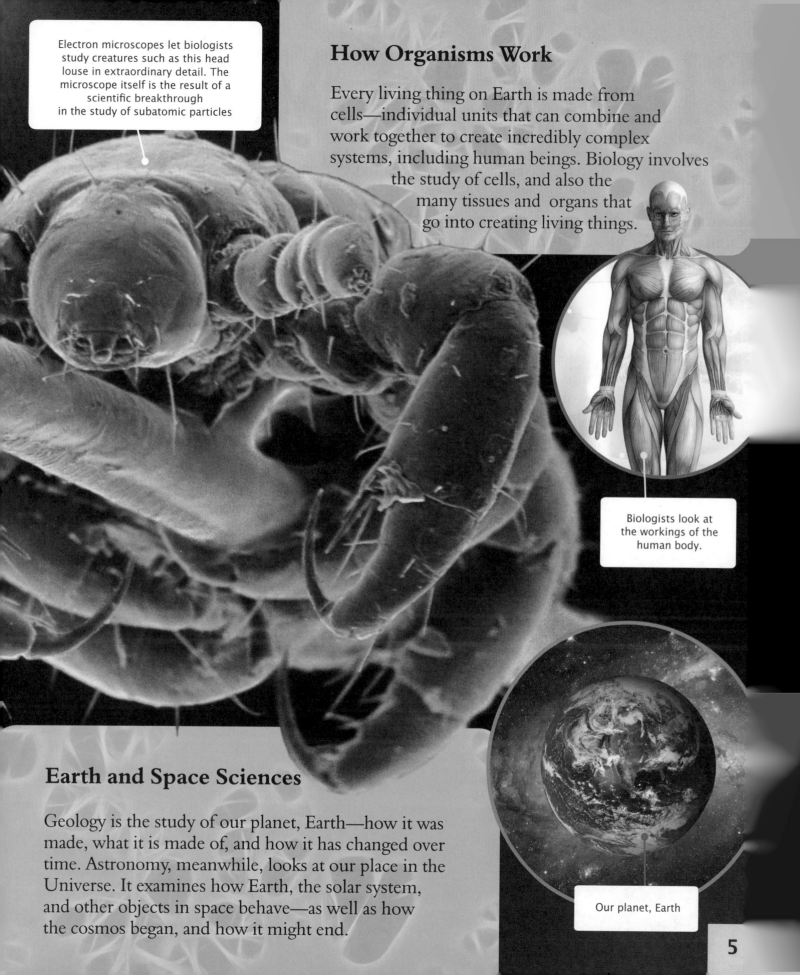

Electron microscopes let biologists study creatures such as this head louse in extraordinary detail. The microscope itself is the result of a scientific breakthrough in the study of subatomic particles

How Organisms Work

Every living thing on Earth is made from cells—individual units that can combine and work together to create incredibly complex systems, including human beings. Biology involves the study of cells, and also the many tissues and organs that go into creating living things.

Biologists look at the workings of the human body.

Earth and Space Sciences

Geology is the study of our planet, Earth—how it was made, what it is made of, and how it has changed over time. Astronomy, meanwhile, looks at our place in the Universe. It examines how Earth, the solar system, and other objects in space behave—as well as how the cosmos began, and how it might end.

Our planet, Earth

Phases of Matter

Matter is the stuff that makes up the Universe. It is built from countless tiny particles called atoms and molecules. Depending on how these particles arrange themselves and join together, matter can take one of three forms: solid, liquid, or gas. These forms are called phases.

Material Bonds

Solid substances are made up of particles joined by strong, rigid bonds. Particles in liquids have looser bonds, which constantly break and reform. Gases are very loose collections of atoms or molecules that have extremely weak bonds. The strength of a material's bonds affects its ability to keep its shape.

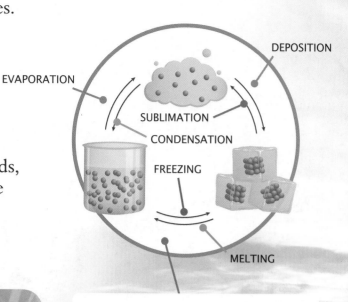

DEPOSITION

EVAPORATION

SUBLIMATION

CONDENSATION

FREEZING

MELTING

Water can be a solid (ice), liquid, or gas (steam). When it's solid, it stays the same shape whatever container it's put in. As a liquid, its molecules flow outward to spread across surfaces. Steam spreads to fill its container or heads in all directions.

Changing Phases

The phase of a substance is affected by how much energy its individual particles have to move around, and this energy depends on the material's temperature. Heating a solid material enough loosens its bonds and makes it melt. Heating a liquid will cause particles to boil or evaporate into a gas.

Different substances have different melting and boiling points. The melting point of rock is very high, so molten lava rapidly turns solid when it erupts from a volcano and begins to cool.

A geyser is created where matter suddenly changes its phase.

As the steam meets the cold air above, it cools and turns back to liquid water droplets.

Wherever the water finds a way through cracks to the surface, it suddenly and violently boils into steam.

Below ground, hot rocks heat liquid water higher than boiling point, but trap it so it cannot turn to steam.

AMAZING DISCOVERY

Scientist: James Thomson
Discovery: Triple point of water
Date: 1873
The story: Thomson was an engineer specializing in water transport. He showed that pure water can coexist as a solid, liquid, and water vapor at a particular pressure and temperature: 0.01°C (32.01°F).

Solid Materials

Most objects are made of solid matter. The atoms or molecules that make up a solid are held together very strongly. There are lots of very different solids, but they all share certain features.

Solid Properties

In some solids, the atoms form regular patterns called crystals. Quartz and salt have a crystal structure. In other solids—for example, polyethylene—the atoms bond in more of a jumble. Some of these shapeless solids can change shape by stretching—this is called being ductile.

A crystal's shape depends on the arrangement of atoms inside. Its hue depends on the elements involved.

The metal iron is ductile. When it's hot, it can be pulled or hammered into shape.

Inside crystals, atoms can be arranged in cubes, hexagons, pyramids, or diamond shapes.

Crystals such as this quartz form by slowly adding new atoms to the outside edges of a growing structure.

Conducting Heat

Solids respond to being heated in different ways. Some solids, including many metals, carry the heat rapidly from one atom to the next. They are called conductors. Others, such as wood or plastic, do not pass on heat. They are called insulators.

In nature, large crystals can can take millions of years to grow. These quartz crystals were grown artificially in just a few hours.

A metal pan conducts heat rapidly through its base to the food inside. However, a wooden spoon (purple and cool in this thermal image) insulates the cook's hand from the heat.

AMAZING DISCOVERY

Scientists: Metalworkers in what is now Turkey
Discovery: Steel
Date: c.2000 BCE
The story: Iron Age metalworkers found that adding other materials to a metal created an alloy that was more useful than the pure metal. For example, people in ancient Turkey found that adding charcoal to iron produced strong steel.

Liquids and Gases

Most substances are only liquid in a narrow range of temperatures, between their solid and gas phases. Atoms or molecules inside liquids are more loosely bonded than those in solids. In gases, their bonds are even weaker.

Moving Particles

In everyday language, we use "fluid" to mean a liquid. In science, it covers both liquids and gases because their particles can flow more or less freely. Water molecules run very freely but those in treacle are more strongly bonded and flow more slowly. Slow-moving, thick liquids are described as "viscous."

Special photography techniques reveal how the molecules in gases or liquids are constantly moving—for example, in this cough.

Gas Laws

Gases expand to fill the space available. If the gas is contained, its molecules will bounce off the walls of its container, producing pressure. Heating a gas speeds up the movement of its molecules and increases its pressure. Pumping air into a bicycle tire increases the pressure of gas inside, and also raises its temperature.

In cooler weather, the gas molecules in the tyre slow down. The pressure reduces and the tIre deflates. It has to be pumped up again.

AMAZING DISCOVERY

Scientist: Daniel Bernoulli
Discovery: Bernoulli's principle
Date: 1738
The story: Swiss mathematician Bernoulli discovered that fluids flowing at fast speeds create less pressure than slow-moving ones. The design of an aircraft wing uses this principle to create lift—its shape forces air to move quickly as it passes over its upper surface.

Hot-air balloons work because hot gases rise up through cooler ones. That's because heat moves through fluids by convection—a process where hot parts of the substance expand and flow into colder areas.

The air in the balloon is warmer and lighter than the surrounding cold air, so the balloon floats upward.

The warm air molecules expand and put pressure on the balloon's inner walls so they bulge outward.

The Story of Life

Our planet is home to nearly nine million species (types of living thing). They range from tiny bacteria to blue whales and from humans to giant redwood trees. Biologists group together species that share characteristics to create a complex "tree of life." They organize living things into five kingdoms: animals, plants, fungi, prokaryotes (bacteria and blue-green algae), and protoctists (such as amoebas).

One Big Family

All living things are descended from a single common ancestor—a simple organism that lived about four billion years ago. This organism's descendants found different ways to survive. They branched out to produce the millions of species on Earth today, as well as countless others along the way.

Bacteria use chemical reactions and cell division to survive and copy themselves. The first living organism did this too.

What is a Species?

Living things belong in the same species if they can breed with each other and produce offspring that can also breed. It's not always possible to test this, but scientists can look for shared genes or body features instead.

Coral reefs, like this one off the island of Fiji in the South Pacific, are home to tens of thousands of species.

Dogs come in an amazing variety of shapes and sizes, but they are a single species. Because their genes are almost identical, different breeds can mate and have puppies.

AMAZING DISCOVERY

Scientist: Carl Linnaeus
Discovery: The tree of life
Date: 1735
The story: Swedish scientist Linnaeus invented a two–name system for classifying every living thing by its genus and species (eg *Homo sapiens* for modern humans). This was the first step toward grouping species in a tree of life.

Scientists collect each group of closely related species together into a genus. Related genera are grouped into families, families into orders, orders into classes, classes into phyla, and phyla into kingdoms.

Three-quarters of all living organisms are found on land.

The green sea turtle, *Chelonia mydas*, belongs to a larger family of sea turtles called the Cheloniidae.

The Story of DNA

Every living thing has its own set of instructions that tells it how to create the chemicals vital to life—and how to put them together. These instructions, called genes, are found inside a long, twisty molecule called DNA (short for deoxyribonucleic acid).

Pairs and Patterns

The DNA molecule looks like a spiral ladder. The ladder's "rungs" are made of pairs of chemicals called bases. The order of the base pairs spells out a code that can be used to build proteins and other chemicals.

The DNA molecule forms a long, winding ladder shape that is called a double helix.

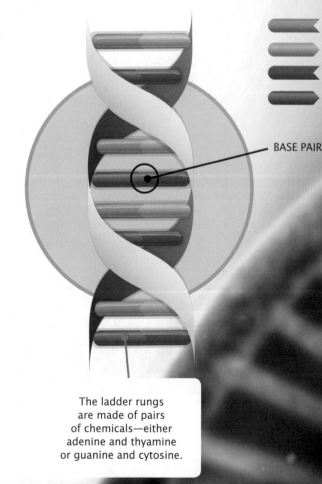

ADENINE

THYMINE

GUANINE

CYTOSINE

BASE PAIR

The ladder rungs are made of pairs of chemicals—either adenine and thyamine or guanine and cytosine.

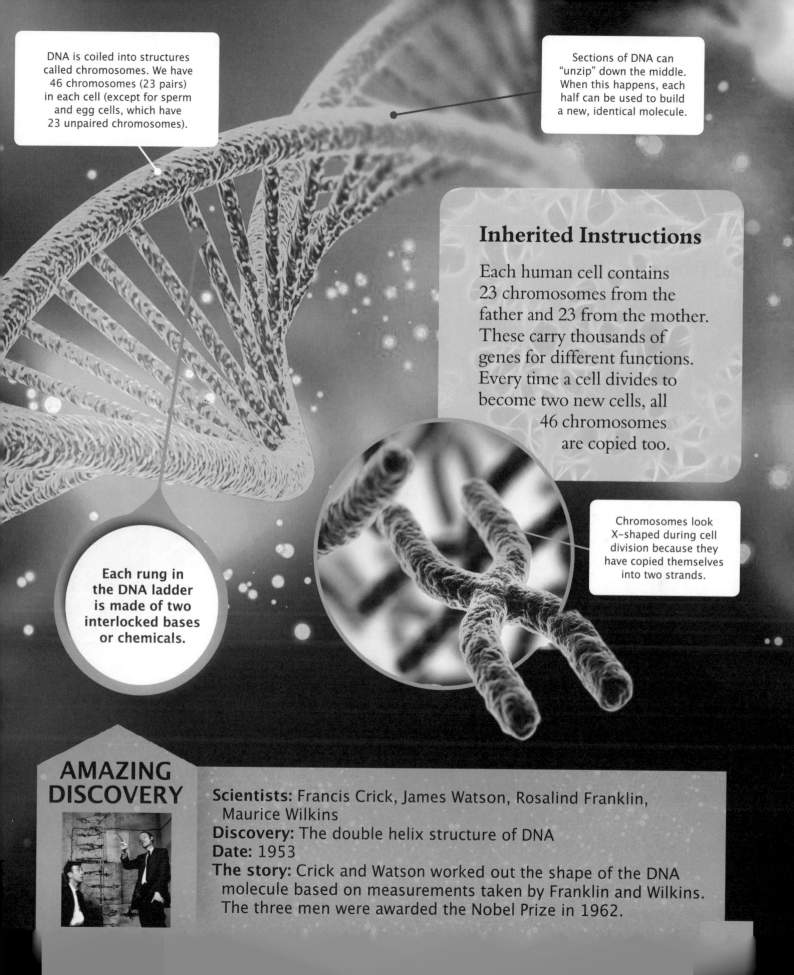

DNA is coiled into structures called chromosomes. We have 46 chromosomes (23 pairs) in each cell (except for sperm and egg cells, which have 23 unpaired chromosomes).

Sections of DNA can "unzip" down the middle. When this happens, each half can be used to build a new, identical molecule.

Inherited Instructions

Each human cell contains 23 chromosomes from the father and 23 from the mother. These carry thousands of genes for different functions. Every time a cell divides to become two new cells, all 46 chromosomes are copied too.

Chromosomes look X-shaped during cell division because they have copied themselves into two strands.

Each rung in the DNA ladder is made of two interlocked bases or chemicals.

AMAZING DISCOVERY

Scientists: Francis Crick, James Watson, Rosalind Franklin, Maurice Wilkins
Discovery: The double helix structure of DNA
Date: 1953
The story: Crick and Watson worked out the shape of the DNA molecule based on measurements taken by Franklin and Wilkins. The three men were awarded the Nobel Prize in 1962.

Plants

There are nearly 400,000 plant species on Earth. Plants are living things that can make their own food. During this process they produce oxygen, the gas that all animals, including humans, must breathe to stay alive.

Food from Sunlight

Plants take in carbon dioxide from the air through their leaves and water from the soil through their roots. Then they use the energy in sunlight to transform these ingredients into sugars. This process, called photosynthesis, is a chemical reaction. It takes place in the leaves, helped by a green chemical called chlorophyll.

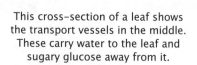

Sequoia trees can live up to 3,000 years. Some other plants live less than a year.

This cross-section of a leaf shows the transport vessels in the middle. These carry water to the leaf and sugary glucose away from it.

Plant Reproduction

Seedless plants, such as liverworts, mosses, and ferns, reproduce by releasing spores. If a spore lands in a suitable place, it produces sex cells and, after fertilization, a new plant can grow. Seed plants produce seeds when male sex cells fertilize female ones. A seed contains a complete embryo plant along with a supply of food.

Pollen contains male sex cells. These must reach other flowers to fertilize their female sex cells. Pollen can be carried by insects and birds that visit the flower to feed on nectar.

Tree trunks are made of cellulose, the tough, fibrous material that forms the cell walls of plants.

To get as much light as possible, plants hold themselves upright using a stem or trunk.

Like all conifers, the sequoia makes its seeds on special scales that are packed together to form cones.

Roots below the ground anchor plants so they don't fall over. They also suck up water and nutrients from the soil.

AMAZING DISCOVERY

Scientist: Jan Ingenhousz
Discovery: Photosynthesis
Date: 1779
The story: This Dutch scientist discovered that plants release different gases if kept in sunlight or darkness. He realized that they absorb carbon dioxide from the atmosphere to build their bodies.

Animals

Animals are living things that get their energy from food, water, oxygen, and the Sun. Unlike plants, they can usually move around in search of food. To harvest energy from their food, animals need to breathe in oxygen.

Animal Types

Fish, amphibians, reptiles, birds, and mammals all have a backbone and skeleton to support their body. They are called vertebrates and make up less than 10 percent of animals. The rest are invertebrates, which don't have a skeleton. They include arthropods, such as insects and spiders, which have a tough outer casing called an exoskeleton, and soft-bodied molluscs.

Symmetry

Most animals have a body plan that is symmetrical—the same on both sides. Features such as limbs and some organs are copied in mirror image. The gut, used to process food, leads from one end of the body to the other.

Centipedes and millipedes

Spiders

Insects

ARTHROPODS

Crustaceans

Annelids

Mollusks

Roundworms

PSEUDOCOELOMATES

ACOELOMATES

Flatworms

Symmetry appears in the very first few cells of a developing animal embryo. It often appears in adult features, such as this tiger's beautiful fur.

Sponges

Scientist: Jennifer Clack
Discovery: *Acanthostega*
Date: 1987
The story: When Clack found a skeleton of *Acanthostega* in Greenland—"Boris"—she realized it was a key step in the evolution of tetrapods (land vertebrates). Boris lived 360 million years and had a fishlike body with four legs. She later found tracks of another early tetrapod.

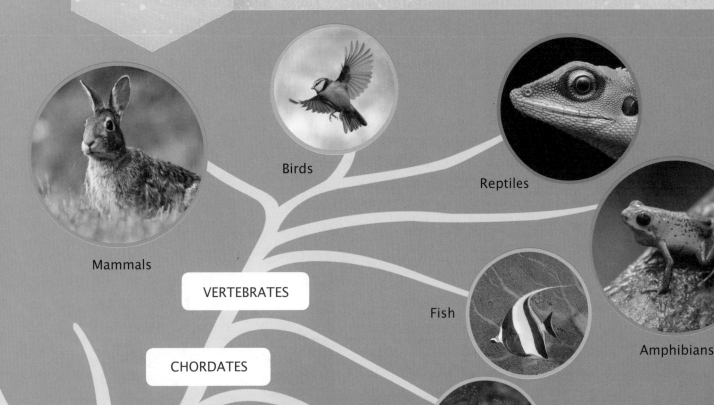

Birds

Reptiles

Mammals

VERTEBRATES

Fish

Amphibians

CHORDATES

DEUTEROSTOMES

Tunicates

PROTOSOMES

COELOMATES

This simple tree shows the different groups in the animal kingdom and how they relate to each other.

Echinoderms

RADIATES

The huge diversity of animals that exist today all evolved from simple one-celled organisms called protists.

ANCESTRAL PROTISTA

Cnidarians

The Human Body

The body is a complex collection of about 37 trillion cells that work together to create a living, thinking human being. Those cells are joined together to make tissues that have different properties. The tissues build up into organs with specific jobs, from pumping blood to making hormones.

Body Systems

The body has systems to look after different functions. Bones and muscles provide support and movement. The brain and nerves gather information about our surroundings and help us to respond. The heart and lungs provide muscles with fuel. The digestive system harvests energy from the food we eat. Other systems repair the body and keep it stable.

OTHER ELEMENTS

NITROGEN

HYDROGEN

CARBON

OXYGEN

Some body systems involve an organ in a particular place, such as the lungs. Others, such as the nervous system, are spread throughout our body.

Human Recipe

We are built from common chemical elements. Oxygen makes up 65 percent of our mass, 9.5 percent is lightweight hydrogen, and 18.5 percent is carbon (a versatile element that builds the complex chemicals necessary for life). Nitrogen, calcium, and phosphorus account for 5.2 percent. The remaining 1.8 percent is made up of tiny amounts of other elements.

Most of our body's oxygen and hydrogen is locked up in water molecules (H_2O). Water makes up 55-60 percent of an adult's body weight, and more in children.

The systems of the body are always working, whether the body is at rest or doing something energetic.

The brain tells the body what to do based on information gathered by the eyes, ears, and other sensory organs.

The digestive system provides the energy to run. It gathers nutrients from food, which the blood carries to every cell.

Bones support the legs, and muscles make it possible for them to move. The directions that make the legs run come from the brain.

Inside the Brain

The human brain is the most complex structure in all of nature. It is packed with 86 billion individual cells called neurons, which form a vast web of connections. These neurons send signals with little bursts of electric charge that are carried by a flow of chemicals washing around the brain.

How the Brain Works

Our brain is split into different regions, each made up of neurons that are specialized to carry out particular tasks. Areas near the middle and bottom of the brain handle instinctive tasks and help regulate our body. The wrinkly outer layer of the brain, called the cerebral cortex, is in charge of more complex tasks such as thinking and sensory processing.

The cerebral cortex's wrinkles give neurons maximum space. The wrinklier the brain, the more processing it can do!

On each side of the cerebral cortex there are four distinct areas called lobes.

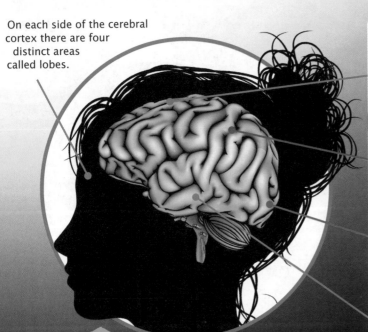

The frontal lobes look after emotions, thinking, memory, planning, language, and more.

The parietal lobes are concerned with the senses of taste and touch.

The occipital lobes are where we process information from our eyes.

The temporal lobes manage our hearing.

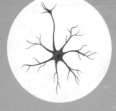

AMAZING DISCOVERY

Scientist: Santiago Ramón y Cajal
Discovery: The neuron doctrine
Date: 1888
The story: Spanish anatomist Ramón y Cajal used new techniques to study neurons under the microscope. He showed that the nervous system was made up of individual nerve cells that formed temporary connections when they were passing on chemical instructions.

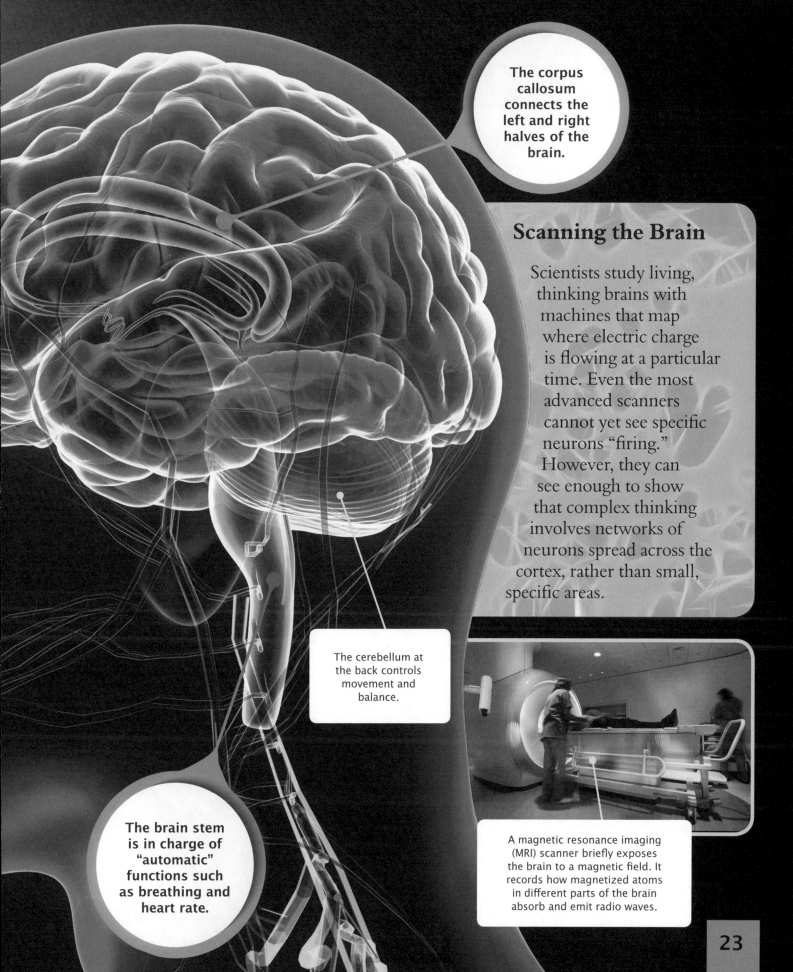

The corpus callosum connects the left and right halves of the brain.

Scanning the Brain

Scientists study living, thinking brains with machines that map where electric charge is flowing at a particular time. Even the most advanced scanners cannot yet see specific neurons "firing." However, they can see enough to show that complex thinking involves networks of neurons spread across the cortex, rather than small, specific areas.

The cerebellum at the back controls movement and balance.

The brain stem is in charge of "automatic" functions such as breathing and heart rate.

A magnetic resonance imaging (MRI) scanner briefly exposes the brain to a magnetic field. It records how magnetized atoms in different parts of the brain absorb and emit radio waves.

Bone and Muscle

Bones are a special type of rigid, hardened tissue that supports the weight of the human body and gives it an overall shape. Cartilage is a tough but flexible connective tissue that holds the framework of bones together. Muscles attached to bones can pull in different directions so our body changes shape and can move.

Our Skeleton

Babies are born with 300 bones in their body, but as we grow some of these join together—most adults have 206. Bones get their toughness from a mineral called calcium phosphate. Despite their solid appearance, bones are spongy inside, and filled with a tissue called marrow that produces the body's blood cells.

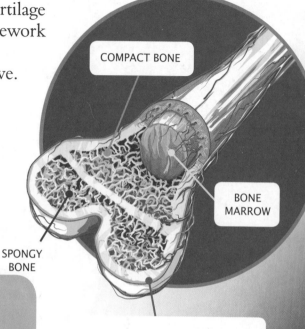

COMPACT BONE

BONE MARROW

SPONGY BONE

Most of our blood cells are manufactured by bone marrow in the large, ball-like ends of long bones such as the femur or hip bone.

Muscle Tissues

Muscles are made up of special cells that can reduce in length, creating a pulling force. Skeletal muscle is the most common type, made up of stringy bundles. Smooth muscle lines blood vessels and various body organs. Cardiac muscle is a special kind of muscle in the heart that can work without resting.

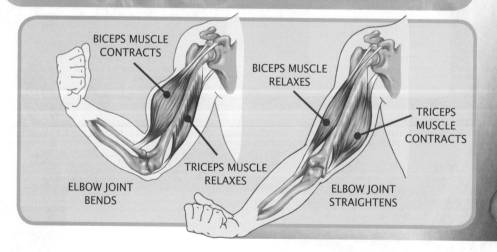

BICEPS MUSCLE CONTRACTS

BICEPS MUSCLE RELAXES

TRICEPS MUSCLE CONTRACTS

TRICEPS MUSCLE RELAXES

ELBOW JOINT BENDS

ELBOW JOINT STRAIGHTENS

Together, the feet contain 52 bones— that's one-quarter of all the bones in the body.

Muscles can only pull, not push, so many skeletal muscles work together in opposing pairs. As one relaxes and the other contracts, they make a joint move.

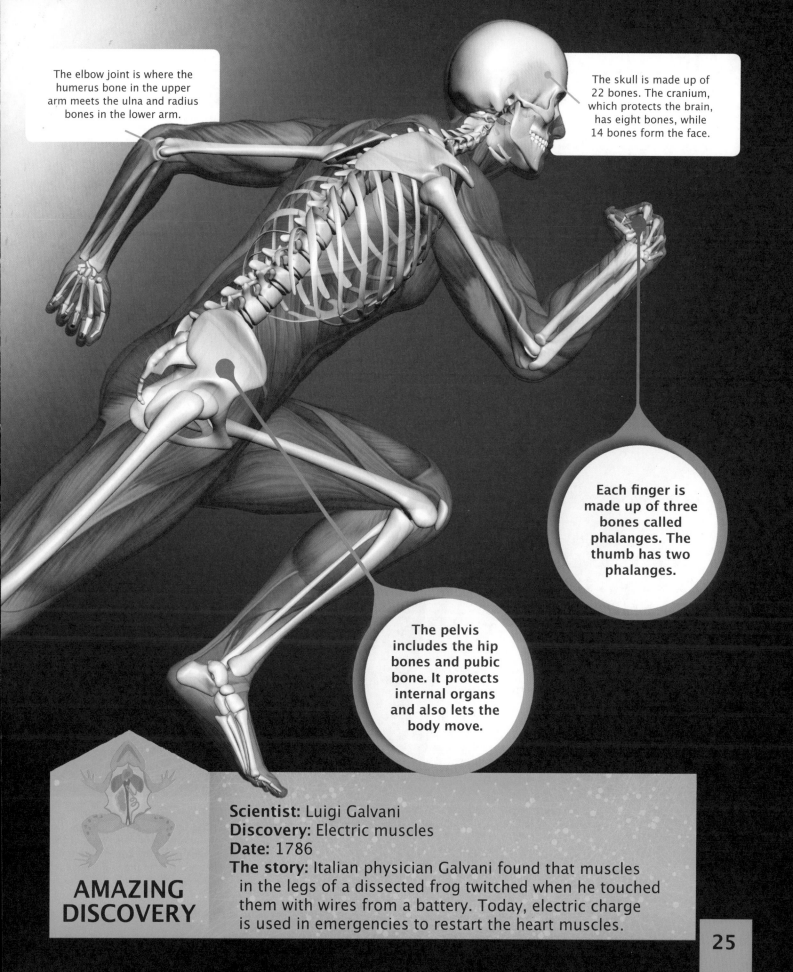

The elbow joint is where the humerus bone in the upper arm meets the ulna and radius bones in the lower arm.

The skull is made up of 22 bones. The cranium, which protects the brain, has eight bones, while 14 bones form the face.

Each finger is made up of three bones called phalanges. The thumb has two phalanges.

The pelvis includes the hip bones and pubic bone. It protects internal organs and also lets the body move.

AMAZING DISCOVERY

Scientist: Luigi Galvani
Discovery: Electric muscles
Date: 1786
The story: Italian physician Galvani found that muscles in the legs of a dissected frog twitched when he touched them with wires from a battery. Today, electric charge is used in emergencies to restart the heart muscles.

Nervous System

The brain and spinal cord make up the central nervous system. They contain neurons—specialized nerve cells that carry information around the brain, and between the brain and body. There are two other kinds of nerve cell—sensory nerves and motor nerves—which look after our senses and movement.

Signals and Synapses

Information travels from neuron to neuron as bursts of electrically charged chemicals. Signals cross tiny gaps between the neurons, called synapses, and enter the next neuron through one of its short tendrils, called dendrites. Signals leave the neuron along its one extra-long tendril, the axon, and cross synapses into other neurons.

On Two Levels

Part of the nervous system works automatically without us having to think about it. It controls organs and body functions, and sends signals to relax the body or prepare it for action. The other part of the nervous system handles tasks that require more complex thought, such as interpreting senses and moving muscles.

The spinal cord is the highway between the body and the brain. Nerves branch off it to every part of the body.

When it is tapped by the doctor's hammer, the knee jerks involuntarily. This is a reflex action. Nearby nerve cells make the knee jerk without waiting for directions from the brain. Reflexes help to protect the body from harm.

The axon is like a long, very thin wire. It carries outgoing electrical signals from the neuron.

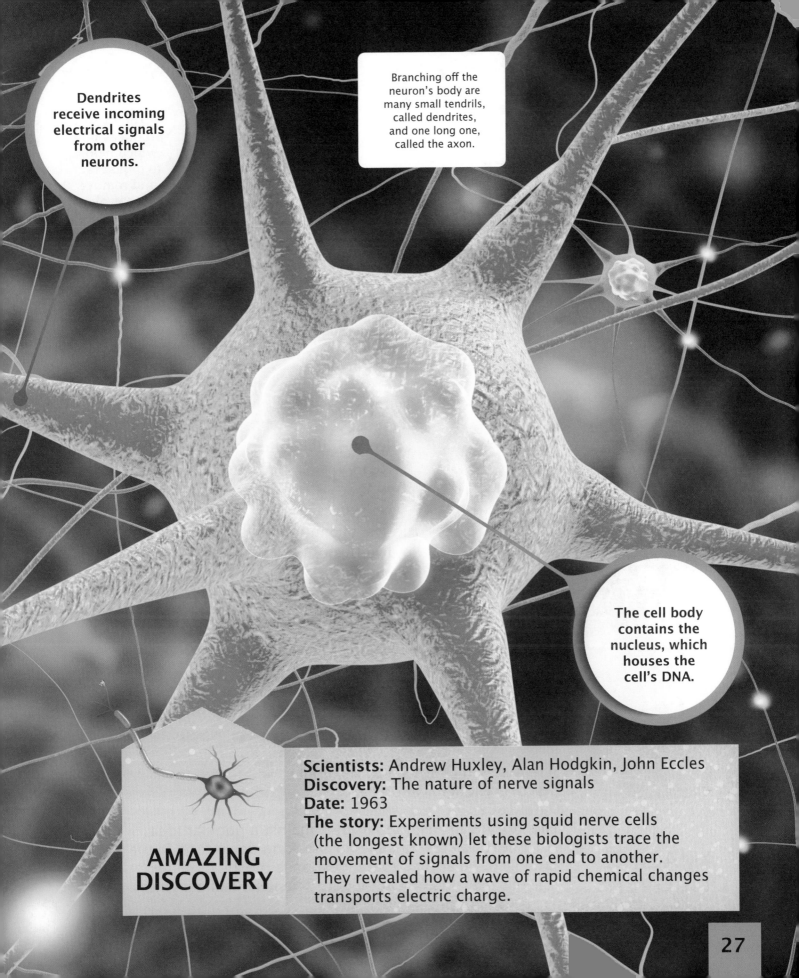

Dendrites receive incoming electrical signals from other neurons.

Branching off the neuron's body are many small tendrils, called dendrites, and one long one, called the axon.

The cell body contains the nucleus, which houses the cell's DNA.

AMAZING DISCOVERY

Scientists: Andrew Huxley, Alan Hodgkin, John Eccles
Discovery: The nature of nerve signals
Date: 1963
The story: Experiments using squid nerve cells (the longest known) let these biologists trace the movement of signals from one end to another. They revealed how a wave of rapid chemical changes transports electric charge.

Digestive System

Like all animals, humans need to harvest energy from food to survive. This process is called digestion. A series of organs, linked to one another along a tube called the gastrointestinal tract (gut), break down the food, remove its useful nutrients, and get rid of any waste.

The liver produces bile, which helps to digest fats and remove cholesterol and other waste products.

In and Out

When we swallow, chewed-up food squeezes down a tube called the gullet or esophagus to the stomach. Here, strong muscles mush up the food and gastric juices begin to break it down. The intestines absorb the nutrients from the food into the bloodstream, leaving behind waste that is pushed out of the rectum.

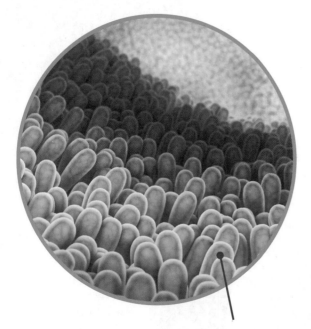

The small intestine is lined with thousands of tiny protrusions called villi. Digested nutrients pass through their thin walls and into the bloodstream.

The large intestine processes the watery waste that leaves the small intestine. It absorbs water back into the bloodstream and creates solid waste—poop.

AMAZING DISCOVERY

Scientist: Jan Baptiste van Helmont
Discovery: Chemical digestion
Date: 1662
The story: Van Helmont argued against a popular idea that heat was responsible for breaking down food in the stomach. He argued that digestion is mostly done by chemical agents—what modern scientists call enzymes.

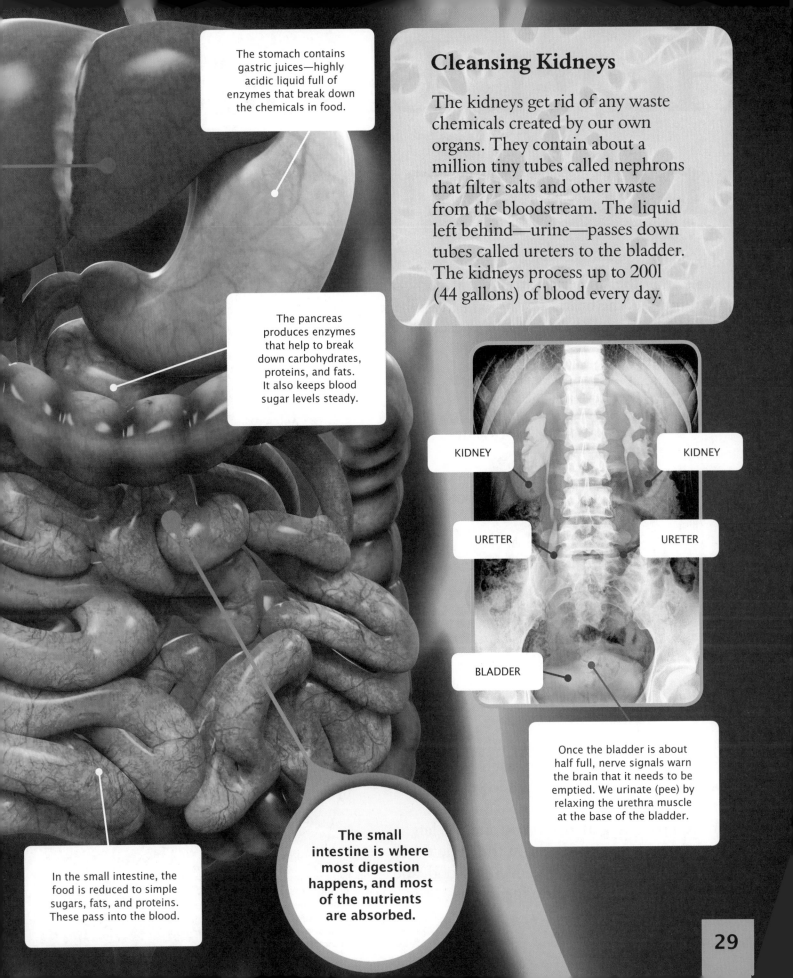

The stomach contains gastric juices—highly acidic liquid full of enzymes that break down the chemicals in food.

Cleansing Kidneys

The kidneys get rid of any waste chemicals created by our own organs. They contain about a million tiny tubes called nephrons that filter salts and other waste from the bloodstream. The liquid left behind—urine—passes down tubes called ureters to the bladder. The kidneys process up to 200l (44 gallons) of blood every day.

The pancreas produces enzymes that help to break down carbohydrates, proteins, and fats. It also keeps blood sugar levels steady.

KIDNEY

KIDNEY

URETER

URETER

BLADDER

Once the bladder is about half full, nerve signals warn the brain that it needs to be emptied. We urinate (pee) by relaxing the urethra muscle at the base of the bladder.

In the small intestine, the food is reduced to simple sugars, fats, and proteins. These pass into the blood.

The small intestine is where most digestion happens, and most of the nutrients are absorbed.

Heart, Blood, and Lungs

Blood is the body's transport system. It moves many different chemicals and other materials around our body, pumped by a powerful muscle, the heart. The blood's most important job is to carry oxygen from the lungs to the muscles so they can work.

Blood is made up of a watery liquid called plasma. Most of it is made up of red blood cells. There are also white blood cells that fight disease and platelets that help blood to clot.

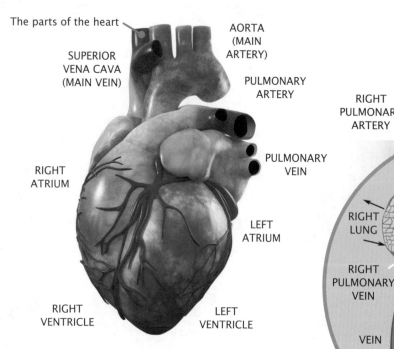

The parts of the heart

SUPERIOR VENA CAVA (MAIN VEIN)

AORTA (MAIN ARTERY)

PULMONARY ARTERY

PULMONARY VEIN

RIGHT ATRIUM

LEFT ATRIUM

LEFT VENTRICLE

RIGHT VENTRICLE

RIGHT PULMONARY ARTERY

HEAD AND ARMS

LEFT PULMONARY ARTERY

RIGHT LUNG

LEFT LUNG

RIGHT PULMONARY VEIN

HEART

LEFT PULMONARY VEIN

LIVER

VEIN

STOMACH

ARTERY

KIDNEYS

TRUNK AND LEGS

The heart pumps blood to the lungs along the pulmonary arteries. Pulmonary veins carry the oxygen–rich blood (red) back to the heart. Arteries take blood to every part of the body and veins carry oxygen–poor blood (blue) back to the heart.

Circulatory System

The heart is a hollow, muscular pump. It has two halves, left and right. Each half has an upper chamber, the atrium, and a lower chamber, the ventricle. During each heartbeat, the left atrium receives oxygen-rich blood and the left ventricle pumps it to the body. At the same time, the right atrium receives oxygen-poor blood, and the right ventricle pumps it to the lungs.

Lung Structure

The lungs are two large sacs filled with branching passages that end in little pouches called alveoli. Tiny capillaries (blood vessels) wrap around the alveoli. Oxygen from air breathed into the lungs can cross the capillary membrane into the bloodstream. Carbon dioxide, a waste gas produced by muscles, can move the other way.

Red blood cells carry oxygen from the lungs and carbon dioxide to the lungs.

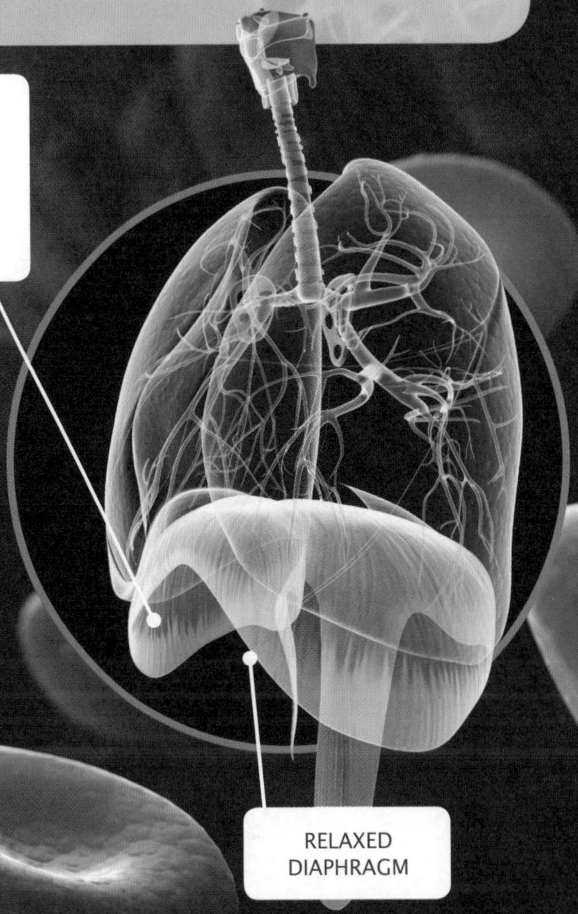

A muscle called the diaphragm helps us to breathe. When it contracts (pulls down), the lungs expand in size and draw in air. When it relaxes (moves up), the lungs are squeezed and air is forced out.

RELAXED DIAPHRAGM

AMAZING DISCOVERY

Scientist: William Harvey
Discovery: Circulation of blood
Date: 1628
The story: Harvey discovered that veins have valves that let blood flow only one way. He realized that the heart pumps blood around the body, and that blood passes from arteries to veins through capillaries that he predicted, but could not see.

Forces and Energy

Scientist Isaac Newton laid the foundations of modern physics with three laws of motion that he identified in the late 1600s. These laws describe the way that objects move, how they react to each other, and how forces can affect their motion.

First and Second Laws

Newton's first law says that objects will always stay still or keep moving with the same velocity (speed in one direction) unless they are affected by a force. His second law states that the bigger that force on the object, the greater the change in its momentum. Momentum is an object's mass times its velocity.

When the downward force of gravity acts on the roller coaster, it changes its momentum.

This cheetah weighs about 74 kg (163 lb), but the bull weighs ten times as much. The cheetah has a top speed or velocity five times faster than the bull, but it still has only half of its momentum.

AMAZING DISCOVERY

Scientist: Isaac Newton
Discovery: Laws of motion
Date: 1679–1687
The story: Philosopher Newton wanted to understand the elongated orbits of comets around the Sun. He realized they were obeying simple laws of motion—they were being influenced by the powerful force of the Sun's gravity.

According to Newton's first law, an object stays as it is unless a force acts on it. The force that gets the rollercoaster started is provided by the mechanical chain that pulls it to its first high point.

The downward stretches of the rollercoaster ride demonstrate Newton's second law. The mass of the cars and riders combines with the force of gravity to make the cars speed up down the track.

As the riders push down on their seats, the seats push back at them in an equal and opposite reaction.

Action and Reaction

Newton's third law of motion is that an object reacts to the force acting on it. The force of this reaction is equal to the original force, but in the opposite direction. If the masses of the two objects are the same, they push away from each other at the same velocity.

When a heavy bat applies force to a lightweight ball, it boosts the ball to high velocity. The bat recoils with a much lower velocity. The velocities aren't equal because the bat and ball have different masses.

33

Heat and Energy

Energy is the ability to do work and make things happen. Energy cannot be created or destroyed, but is always changing from one form to another. Heat is a form of energy that makes the individual atoms in a material vibrate or jostle around. Other types of energy often get "lost" as heat, and then can't be recovered.

Forms of Energy

Energy can take many forms. Moving objects have kinetic energy. Potential energy is energy that is stored and ready to be used to do work in the future. Chemical energy is released when bonds form in a chemical reaction.

This is a Newton's cradle. The three balls on the right have no potential energy and no kinetic energy. The ball on the left has potential energy, because it has been lifted, but no kinetic energy. When the boy releases the ball, it will move and have kinetic energy.

Heat Transfer

There are three main ways that heat energy moves from one place to another. Conduction happens in solids. The energy travels from one atom to the next. Metals conduct heat better than wood. Convection happens in liquids and gases. It is a circular movement where hot areas expand and flow into cooler ones. Heat also travel as infrared.

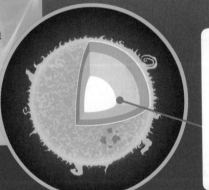

The Sun moves heat in all three ways. Conduction takes the energy from atom to atom. Convection makes hotter particles expand and rise to take the place of ones with less energy. Radiation carries the heat away into space.

AMAZING DISCOVERY

Scientists: Sadi Carnot and others
Discovery: Entropy
Date: 1824–1897
The story: In the 1800s engineers and physicists discovered that it's impossible to move energy from one form to another without losing some, often as heat. The lost energy can no longer do useful work, a state called entropy.

A single flash of lightning releases around five billion joules of energy.

Lightning heats the surrounding air to temperatures of more than 27,000°C (48,632°F).

A lightning strike has four main types of energy: electrical energy, heat, light, and sound.

Secrets of Light

Light is a form of energy that travels as a series of tiny waves. Most of our light comes from the Sun or from electric lights. It moves extremely fast—in fact, nothing in the Universe can travel faster than the speed of light.

Seeing Light

Light is a mix of wavelengths, which our eyes see as different colors. Red light has the longest wavelengths, and blue and violet have the shortest. A red T-shirt looks red because dye molecules in the fabric absorb light from the blue-violet end of the spectrum, and only red light is reflecting back.

At night, when light from the Sun does not reach us, we use artificial electric lighting. The first electric street lights were invented in 1875.

What we see as white light is made up of many hues. When white light passes through a prism, we can see this visible spectrum, which has blue and red at opposite ends.

AMAZING DISCOVERY

Scientist: Isaac Newton
Discovery: The spectrum of visible light
Date: 1672
The story: Newton split a beam of sunlight into a spectrum (rainbow) using a prism, and then brought that spectrum back together to form white light. He showed for the first time that the prism was not somehow "adding" the different hues to light.

Tricks with Light

Light travels in a straight line from its source and bounces off objects (which lets us see them). Microscopes and telescopes use lenses to refract (bend) light and mirrors to reflect it. They can gather more light than our eyes alone, and also produce magnified images.

Hilton Grand Vacations

A magnifying glass bends the paths of light rays coming from the words. It creates a closer and larger virtual version of the words.

The light is behind this tree, which means the area in front of the tree will be in shadow.

Lights make our cities safer, but they also stop us from being able to see the night sky.

Neon lights are tubes containing neon, an element that is a gas. When electricity passes through the gas, it gives off light in a particular color.

Computers

At its most basic, a computer is a device that does simple calculations very quickly, even for very large numbers, and identifies patterns in the numbers. By adding clever design and programming to this basic mathematical ability, we now have computers that can carry out a mind-boggling variety of different tasks.

The Brain

The computer's central processing unit (CPU) "reads" information stored in the computer's memory, performs calculations, and then "writes" results back to other parts of the memory. Electronic components called logic gates let the CPU do mathematics and make decisions based on binary numbers (strings of 1s and 0s).

Although computers are great for games, they can also make difficult and repetitive tasks much easier.

Built between 1943 and 1946, room–sized ENIAC was one of the first digital computers. It could carry out 5,000 instructions a second.

AMAZING DISCOVERY

Scientists: Charles Babbage, Ada Lovelace
Discovery: The analytical engine
Date: 1837, 1843
The story: In 1837, long before electronics, English inventor Babbage designed a universal computing machine using brass wheels. It was never built, but mathematician Lovelace worked out the commands needed to run it, making her the first computer programmer. She published her findings in 1843.

Computer Memory

Computers store information they need fast access to on memory chips. Basic operating instructions are written on permanent Read-Only Memory (ROM) chips. Less urgent data, such as applications or the user's files, is saved on a slower magnetic hard disc and then moved to faster Random Access Memory (RAM) chips when it's needed.

Special computer circuits can create sounds from digital files.

A computer's motherboard connects up all of its various components, including the CPU, ROM, and RAM memory chips, and hard disk drive.

Special graphics processors (GPUs) create realistic moving images on the screen.

A mouse lets the computer user highlight and manipulate items on the screen.

Nanotechnology

Imagine machines made up of individual atoms, able to copy themselves, assemble objects, and even repair our bodies or fight disease at a molecular level. This is the idea behind nanotechnology—and while this new science hasn't yet delivered all these dreams, it is already starting to affect our everyday lives.

Teeny-Tiny Tech

Nanotechnology involves building on the scale of nanometers (billionths of 1 m/3.3 ft) or less. Nanomaterials are substances with engineered atomic-scale structures that give them useful properties. We already use them to make self-cleaning glass, dirt-repellent paints and sprays, and superfine filters for purifying water and trapping viruses.

Carbon nanotubes can be used in touch-screen devices, such as tablets, and high-strength bullet-proof vests.

Building with Atoms

Nanoengineers can also build structures out of individual atoms. They use a machine called an atomic force microscope to "see" the separate atoms on a material—and they can even pick them up and move them around! This technology could eventually let us build complex computers atom by atom.

Scanning tunneling microscopes are the best way of mapping and building with single atoms.

AMAZING DISCOVERY

Scientists: Richard Smalley, Robert Curl, Harold Kroto
Discovery: Fullerenes
Date: 1985
The story: Smalley, Curl, and Kroto led a team of chemists who discovered a ball of carbon atoms that they called buckminsterfullerene. This was the first hint that carbon could create strong rings and tubes for use in nanotechnology.

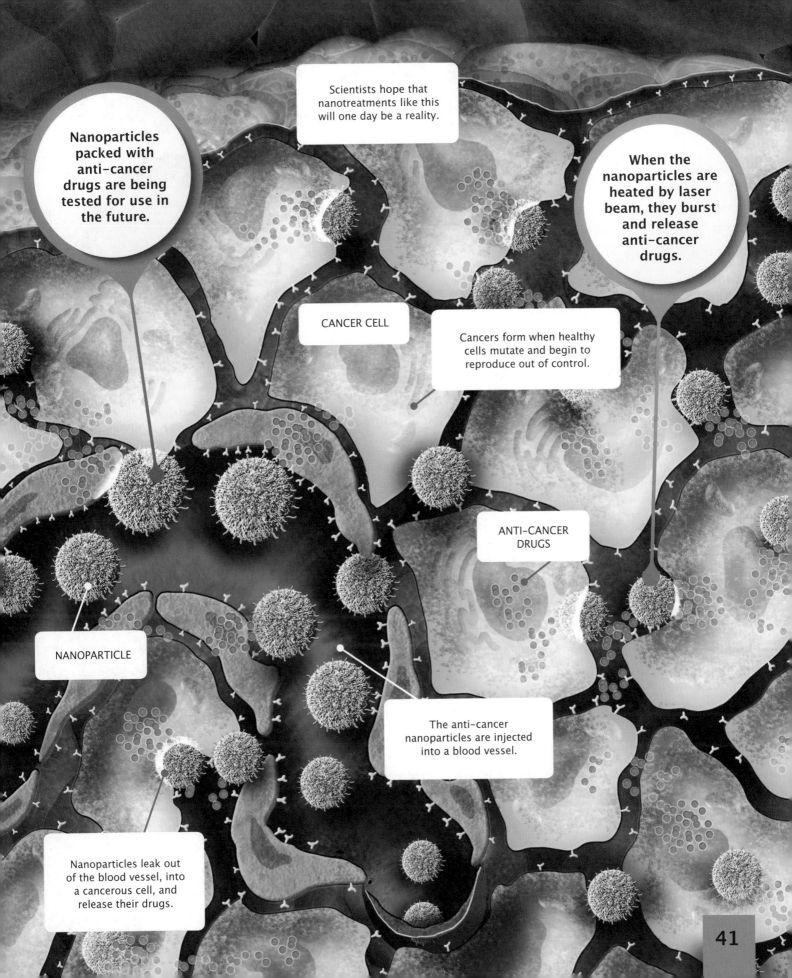

Inside the Earth

Our planet is a huge ball of rock, 12,742 km (7,918 miles) across. It might seem solid all the way through, but not far beneath the surface is a deep layer called the mantle, which is a mix of semi-molten and solid rock. Deeper still, Earth's core is a swirling ball of molten and solid metal.

Layers within Layers

Earth's crust floats on the upper, semi-molten part of the mantle, and is cracked into giant plates. Rocks churn and grind past each other in the mantle, carrying heat from the core to the surface. The superhot core is made of iron and nickel, and mostly molten but solid at its heart.

Earth was born about 4.6 billion years ago out of material left over from making the Sun. At first, even the surface was hot, molten rock. Our planet has been slowly cooling down ever since.

Earth's Magnetic Field

The liquid part of Earth's metal core produces huge electric currents as it swirls, and these create a magnetic field. It is as if our planet were a giant magnet, with magnetic north and south poles close to the axis of its spin. This magnetic field forms a bubble around the Earth, which we call the magnetosphere.

The magnetosphere repels dangerous particles from the Sun. Harmless, lower-energy solar particles fall into the atmosphere over the magnetic poles to create aurorae.

AMAZING DISCOVERY

Scientist: Andrija Mohorovicic
Discovery: Earth's internal layers
Date: 1909
The story: Scientist Mohorovicic observed that earthquake shockwaves change their speed depending on their depth below the surface. He realized this was because they passed through different rock types and temperatures.

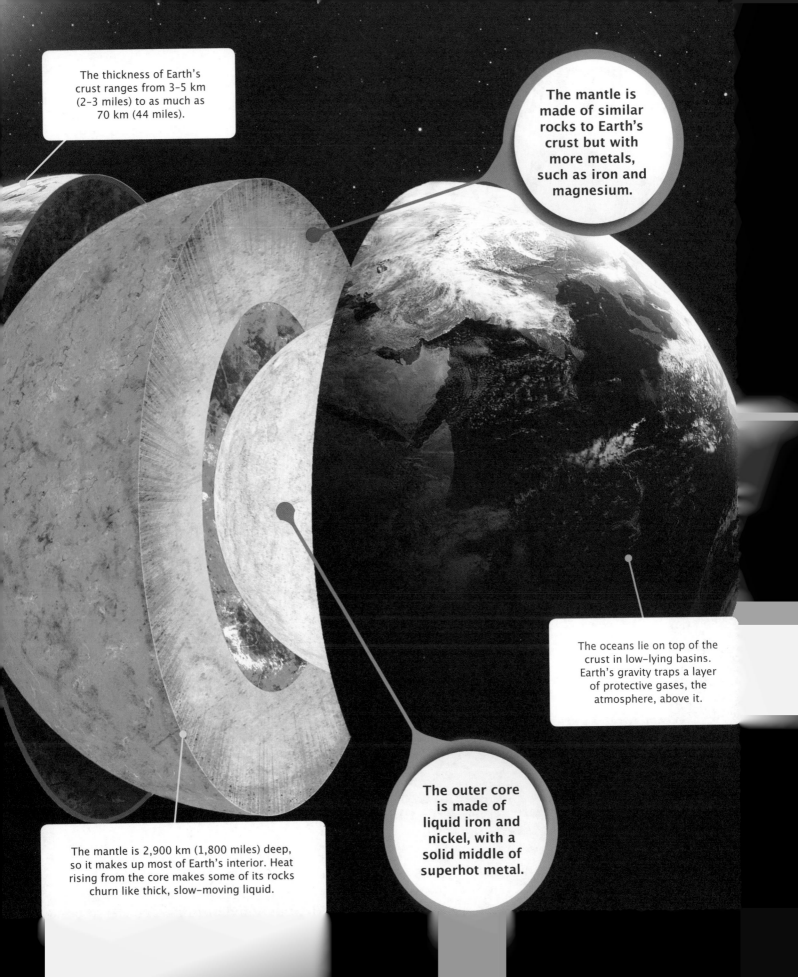

The thickness of Earth's crust ranges from 3–5 km (2–3 miles) to as much as 70 km (44 miles).

The mantle is made of similar rocks to Earth's crust but with more metals, such as iron and magnesium.

The oceans lie on top of the crust in low-lying basins. Earth's gravity traps a layer of protective gases, the atmosphere, above it.

The outer core is made of liquid iron and nickel, with a solid middle of superhot metal.

The mantle is 2,900 km (1,800 miles) deep, so it makes up most of Earth's interior. Heat rising from the core makes some of its rocks churn like thick, slow-moving liquid.

Atmosphere and Weather

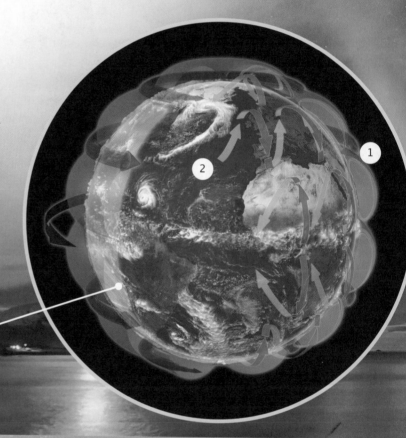

Space particles collide with atoms of gases in the atmosphere, give them energy, and make them glow.

Earth is surrounded by a thin but vital layer of gas called the atmosphere. It provides the air we breathe, creates a protective blanket that keeps out the worst extremes of hot and cold, and gives us a complex system of ever-changing weather.

Atmospheric Gases

Without an atmosphere absorbing and trapping the Sun's heat, our planet would be unbearably hot in the day and icy-cold at night. The main gases in the atmosphere are nitrogen and oxygen. Oceans, rocks, and life absorb and produce different gases, creating a delicate balance.

Weather happens in the troposphere, the layer of the atmosphere that is closest to the Earth.

1. Warm air rises near the equator, cools, and sinks down closer to poles.

2. Winds are driven by the Earth's rotation, and by rising and falling air.

AMAZING DISCOVERY

Scientist: George Hadley
Discovery: Atmospheric circulation and winds
Date: 1735
The story: Amateur meteorologist (weather scientist) Hadley was the first person to realize that wind patterns were due to the Earth spinning on its axis and the way air rises in hot areas and sinks in colder ones.

Aurorae, also known as the northern and southern lights, happen close to the poles. Earth's magnetic field attracts tiny particles from space.

Oxygen atoms glow green at low altitudes and red at high ones. Nitrogen produces blue or purple.

Most aurorae are in the thermosphere. They happen 80-640 km (50-400 miles) above the ground.

Balancing the Climate

Carbon dioxide (CO_2) is called a greenhouse gas because it traps heat like the glass of a greenhouse. The CO_2 in our atmosphere keeps our planet warm. However, burning fossil fuels such as coal and oil creates more CO_2 than there used to be. This is heating the planet at a faster rate and changing our climate.

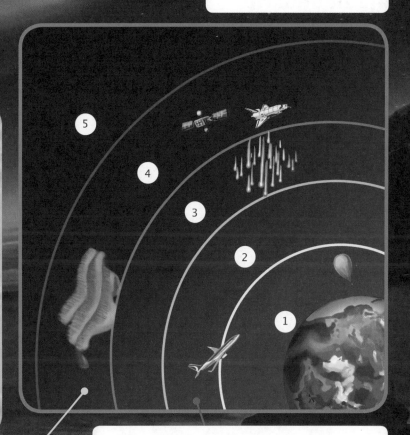

The atmosphere is divided into layers that stretch out into space. It gets thinner the higher we go.

1. TROPOSPHERE up to 12 km (7.5 miles)
2. STRATOSPHERE 12-50 km (7.5-31 miles)
3. MESOSPHERE 50-80 km (31-50 miles)
4. THERMOSPHERE 80-700 km (50-435 miles)
5. EXOSPHERE 700-10,000 km (435-6,214 miles)

Volcanoes and Earthquakes

Powerful forces are unleashed in places where the plates of Earth's crust come together. Huge masses of rock crumple against or grind past each other and trigger devastating earthquakes. Where crust is driven down into the mantle, molten rock escapes through chains of volcanoes.

Violent eruptions happen when trapped gas bursts from pockets of magma beneath Earth's surface.

Plate Boundaries

If plates meet head-on, what happens next depends on the types of crust involved. Thin ocean crust will be pushed under thick continental crust, and as it melts in the mantle it will release heat that creates volcanoes. Where two continental plates meet, they buckle to create towering mountain ranges.

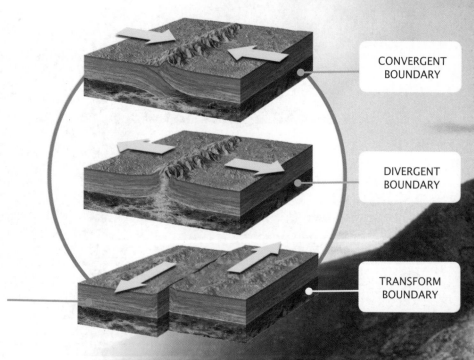

CONVERGENT BOUNDARY

DIVERGENT BOUNDARY

TRANSFORM BOUNDARY

Plates collide at convergent boundaries, pull apart (often beneath the oceans) at divergent boundaries, and grind past each other at transform boundaries.

AMAZING DISCOVERY

Scientist: Alfred Wegener
Discovery: Tectonic drift
Date: 1912
The story: Meteorologist Wegener noticed how the edges of widely separated landmasses fit together like a jigsaw puzzle. He suggested that continents move slowly around on Earth's crust, but his idea only began to be accepted in the 1950s.

Volcanoes form where tectonic movements heat and melt underground rock to form molten magma. When magma erupts at the surface, it is called lava.

Earthquakes

When Earth's crust suddenly shifts, it triggers waves of disturbance called earthquakes. This can happen when tectonic plates collide or when they grind sideways past each other. The waves spread through the crust and also down through the Earth. Sometimes the vibrations can be detected on the other side of the world.

Many of our biggest cities, such as Mexico City, are built in earthquake zones. Unfortunately scientists cannot yet predict exactly where or when a disastrous quake will strike.

Liquid lava from volcanoes cools down rapidly. It solidifies into new igneous rocks.

Volcanoes and earthquakes happen at plate boundaries, and also above random "hot spots" in Earth's mantle.

Glossary

ALLOY
A mixture of two or more metals, or of a metal and a nonmetal.

ATOM
The smallest unit of an element.

BINARY
A base-2 system of numbering—it has only two numbers, 0 and 1. (Our usual numbering system is base-10: 0, 1, 2, 3, 4, 5, 6, 7, 8, 9.)

CELL
The smallest unit of a living body.

DIGITAL
Using signals or information that are in a coded form, usually binary.

DNA (deoxyribonucleic acid)
A substance with the structure of a double helix that carries genes and is found in the nucleus of cells in all living things.

ELECTRIC CHARGE
A property of some forms of matter that means they can be influenced by electromagnetism.

ELECTRICITY
A flow of electric charge from one place to another. It can be harnessed to do work.

ELECTRONICS
A technology that uses the flow of very small electric currents to store, send, and alter information.

ELEMENT
A substance that is made entirely from one type of atom.

ENZYME
A protein that controls a chemical reaction.

FORCE
A push or pull on another object that changes its movement.

GAS
A phase of matter in which atoms or molecules are widely separated and move freely.

GENE
An instruction on a section of a DNA molecule that is needed to make the structures and provide the functions that a living organism requires.

GRAVITY
A force that draws objects that have mass toward each other.

LIQUID
A phase of matter in which atoms or molecules are loosely bound together but can move freely.

LOGIC GATE
Part of a circuit in a computer that decides whether to allow a current through, based on binary numbers.

MAGNETIC FIELD
A form of electromagnetism created around, and felt by, electrical conductors and metals with certain properties.

MINERAL
A solid chemical compound, often with a crystal structure, formed from natural chemicals in water or the ground.

MOLECULE
The smallest unit of a compound, made of two or more atoms bonded together.

NUCLEUS
The middle of an atom, where its positive electric charge and nearly all of its mass are concentrated in a cluster of subatomic particles called protons and neutrons.

ORGAN
A collection of tissues in a complex living thing (usually an animal) that carries out a special function to help the organism survive.

PHOTOSYNTHESIS
A chemical reaction used by plants to make useful chemicals with energy from sunlight, carbon dioxide, and water.

REACTION
A chemical process that breaks apart chemical bonds within molecules, moves atoms around, and creates new molecules.

SOLID
A phase of matter in which atoms or molecules are tightly bound together and cannot move freely.

TISSUE
A collection of cells that carries out a function in a living organism.